LifeTimes

The Story of Wolfgang Amadeus Mozart

by Stewart Ross

illustrated by Alan Marks

Thameside Press

US publication copyright © 2002 Thameside Press.
International copyright reserved in all countries.
No part of this book may be reproduced in any form
without written permission from the publisher.

Distributed in the United States by
Smart Apple Media
1980 Lookout Drive
North Mankato, MN 56003

Produced for Thameside Press by
White-Thomson Publishing Ltd
2/3 St Andrew's Place
Lewes, BN7 1UP, England.

© White-Thomson Publishing Limited 2002
Text copyright © Stewart Ross 2002
Illustrations copyright © Alan Marks 2002

ISBN 1-931983-14-3

Library of Congress Control Number 2002 141328

Editor: Kay Barnham
Designer: John Jamieson
Language consultant: Norah Granger, Senior Lecturer in Primary
    Education, University of Brighton, England.
Music consultant: Roland Vernon

Printed in China

Introduction

Wolfgang Amadeus Mozart was born on January 27 1756, in Salzburg, Austria. His father gave him his first music lessons just three years later. It was soon clear that the young Wolfgang was a musical genius. At the age of five, he performed in public and wrote his first compositions.

In 1791, Wolfgang was living in Vienna with his wife, Constanze. He had written an extraordinary amount of wonderful music and was very famous. However, he was not wealthy and he was not in the best of health. . . .

A Generous Offer

"Hurry up, man!" called the passenger from his carriage window. "I'm due there at ten o'clock!"

"All right, sir!" replied the driver angrily. "I'm doing my best!" He cracked his whip over the horses' backs, and the carriage jerked sharply forward.

The passenger was thrown heavily back into his seat. "Drat that man!" he muttered, picking up his hat from the carriage floor.

"If I say nothing we creep like a lame donkey; if I tell him to speed up he sets off as if the devil were after us!"

A few minutes later, the carriage had once again slowed to a walk. This time the passenger just sighed and stared idly out of the window. "Young Mozart will have to wait," he said to himself. "He won't mind—not when he sees what I've got to offer him!"

The man in the coach was Emanuel
Schikaneder, a wealthy actor, director, and
theater owner. Life was treating him well.
He was in good health, the weather was warm
for mid-March, and his Free House Theater
was packed every night.

Schikaneder smiled as he tapped the bundle
of papers beside him. And now, he thought,
I have this new show, the best ever. If the
music's good, it's bound to be a hit.

That was why Schikaneder needed Mozart.

The 35-year-old composer was the most talented in Vienna, maybe even in Europe. If he wrote the music for Schikaneder's show, it could not fail.

Schikaneder was let into the Mozarts' apartment by the maid, Sabine. "A gentleman to see you, Mrs. Mozart," she announced, showing him into the living room.

Constanze Mozart's round face lit up. "Mr. Schikaneder!" she beamed. "Come in!" She called out, "Wolfgang! Mr. Schikaneder has come to see us!"

Wolfgang Amadeus Mozart was a small man with a big nose and a shock of light-colored hair. Running into the room like an excited schoolboy, he grasped his old friend by the hand.

"Emanuel!" he cried. "Fantastic to see you!" Without a pause, he called, "Sabine, a bottle of wine!" He turned to Constanze. "Isn't this wonderful, darling? A great surprise!"

"It wasn't meant to be a surprise, Wolfgang," smiled Schikaneder. "I did write to say that I was coming."

"Really?" exclaimed Wolfgang. "Oh, dear! Well, you know how inefficient I am. I'm so sorry!"

"Never mind. I've come to ask you a favor," explained Schikaneder.

Wolfgang's eyes lit up. A favor usually meant money, which was good news. It was some time since he'd been well paid for a piece of music.

"I'd like you to compose the music for my new opera," Schikaneder continued. He held out the papers he had brought with him. "It's called *The Magic Flute*."

An opera is a play in which most or all of the words are sung rather than spoken. Operas can be comic or serious. In Mozart's time, they had been performed for about 200 years.

By 1791, Mozart had already written several operas. At least five of them (including *The Marriage of Figaro* and *Don Giovanni*) were outstanding works that are still enjoyed all over the world today.

Worrying Signs

Schikaneder stayed for about an hour. As soon as he was gone, Wolfgang grabbed Constanze by the hands and began whirling her around the room.

"We're go-ing to be rich! We're go-ing to be rich!" he sang in his high, lively voice. "Tra-la-la! We're go-ing to be rich!"

After three twirls, Constanze managed to pull away from her husband. "Careful, Wolfgang!" she exclaimed, sitting gingerly on the couch.

Wolfgang looked suddenly ashamed. He stopped dancing and sat down beside his wife. Of course he had not forgotten she was pregnant, he said, but sometimes he got so carried away. . . .

This was the sixth time in nine years that Constanze had been pregnant. Only one son, seven-year-old Karl Thomas, had survived infancy. The constant strain had made the dark-eyed Constanze look older than her twenty-eight years. Now, she often complained of feeling ill. Her doctor's bills were enormous.

The Mozarts loved dressing in the finest silk clothes and visiting Vienna's most expensive hairdressers. Then there was the rent to pay, and Karl's school fees, and Wolfgang's travel. . . .

"Don't worry, my little honeypot!" he smiled, taking Constanze's hands and kissing the tip of her nose. "Emanuel has offered me 200 ducats to write the music for *The Magic Flute*. That's a whole year's rent!"

Constanze smiled weakly. "You'll only get paid if you're fit enough to work, Wolfgang. You haven't been well for weeks."

A frown settled over her husband's face. "I don't feel terrific. . . . but it won't last, my angel"—the frown faded as quickly as it had come— "and then we'll be as rich as the emperor!"

Wolfgang had no regular job. His only certain income at this time was the 350 ducats a year he received as a court composer for the emperor of Austria. He earned extra money by composing music for anyone prepared to pay him.

The Mozarts had business expenses as well as household bills to pay. Wolfgang had to travel to give concerts and meet patrons, and he was always expected to be well dressed for public performances.

The Summer House

Wolfgang soon started work on *The Magic Flute*. He never found it difficult to compose music. Tunes floated into his head like beautiful dreams, and he knew by instinct the best way to arrange them.

It was as if music were somehow trapped inside him. All he had to do was concentrate a little, and it came pouring out.

The trouble was, Wolfgang was not good at concentrating. If someone came along and offered him a few ducats for a new piece of work, he would forget about *The Magic Flute* and start the other project.

Constanze and he loved billiards. Wolfgang would spend hours sinking billiard balls when he should have been composing.

By the end of May, Schikaneder was getting worried. Would Wolfgang finish the new opera on time?

The composer and the theater owner were sitting at a table outside the Free House Theater. Schikaneder was frowning.

"You're letting me down, Wolfgang," he sighed. "Where's my opera, eh?"

Wolfgang's face lightened. "Oh! Is that all!" he exclaimed. "I thought it was something serious. Listen, Emanuel, I could write *The Magic Flute* in a week if I had to!"

"Rubbish!" snorted Schikaneder. "Anyway, you won't get the chance. From now on I want you working here. Every day."

"Here? In the theater?" Wolfgang looked confused.

"Not in the theater," explained Schikaneder. "In the summer house. It's the perfect place for composing—and there's no billiard table to tempt you away from your work!"

"But I can't work in the summer—" wailed Wolfgang.

"Yes, you can!" interrupted Schikaneder. "You can—and you *must!*"

Schikaneder and the Mozarts lived in Vienna, the capital of the Austrian Empire. It was ruled by the Emperor Joseph II. His sister, Marie Antoinette, was the queen of France.

There had been a revolution in France in 1789. Joseph was worried about his sister's safety and was thinking of going to war with France. To save money for this war, he was spending less on court entertainment. That meant less money for Mozart.

Wolfgang found it
much easier to work in the summer
house. To make sure that he didn't sneak home,
Schikaneder visited him every morning.
Worried that Wolfgang looked unwell, the
kindly theater owner often took him for
a drink or a meal at a local pub.

Amazingly, Wolfgang still found the energy
to write songs and other pieces. His efforts
were extraordinary—and very, very tiring.

Finally, by the beginning of July, all of the
important parts of *The Magic Flute* were finished.

When Schikaneder read it through—the soaring choruses, the sparkling solos, the brilliant orchestral work—his eyes filled with tears. "This is heavenly, Wolfgang," he breathed. "It really is from heaven."

When Constanze gave birth to a healthy baby boy—Franz Xaver—Wolfgang's joy was complete. His wife went to Baden for a short vacation and he stayed in Vienna to regain his strength.

Not long after Constanze and Franz Xaver
had left, the doctor came to visit Wolfgang.
He examined him carefully but could find
nothing wrong.

"You've probably been overdoing it," he said.
"You must rest for a week or so, then you'll
feel much better."

Wolfgang was not so sure.

The following morning, he got up late.
After a hearty breakfast, he sat down to finish
some violin parts for *The Magic Flute*. His desk
overlooked the street, and from time to time he
stopped work and stared out the window.

Shortly before noon, a large, black carriage drew up outside his front door. As Mozart watched, a man got out. Although it was a hot day, a shiver ran down Wolfgang's spine.

The man was dressed all in black, as if he were going to a funeral.

In Mozart's day, medicine was very unscientific. Most doctors had no proper training, and their treatments were often painful and dangerous. It was fairly common, for example, to cut open a patient's vein and let a quantity of blood flow out. Baden, where Constanze went after the birth of Franz Xaver, was a spa town, famous for its healthy spring water.

Like a Shadow

The doorbell rang, and Wolfgang heard Sabine hurrying downstairs to answer it. A moment later, her quick steps approached his study.

"Please, Mr. Mozart, there's a man to see you."

"Show him in, Sabine," Wolfgang replied. He wanted to find out who the gloomy stranger was.

The man in black was tall with a long face, deep-set eyes, and dusty hair flecked with gray.

He slipped into the study noiselessly, as if he were a shadow.

"Mr. Mozart?" he asked in a deep voice that boomed like the inside of a cathedral.

"Yes," replied Wolfgang, stretching out his hand. The stranger grasped it weakly, then let it drop. "And who are you, sir?"

"My name is not important," replied the echoing voice. "I have come to ask you to write a requiem mass."

Wolfgang was startled. A requiem mass was sung for the soul of someone who had died. The thought of writing one now, when he was so unwell, was sinister.

The stranger never gave his name. His master wanted Mozart—and only Mozart—to write a requiem mass. If Wolfgang agreed, he would receive 30 ducats immediately and more when the work was finished.

"Who is your master?" asked Wolfgang.

"That, sir, I may not tell you," boomed the stranger.

"Very well, but can you tell me whose soul this requiem is for?"

"No, sir. That too is secret."

"Well," replied Wolfgang, "this is such a strange request that I must think it over."

The visitor promised to return in a few days. After he left, Wolfgang wrote to Constanze. She urged him to accept the work.

So, when the stranger came back, Wolfgang reluctantly agreed to write a requiem.

Lying in bed that night, Wolfgang realized that the thought of the nameless requiem was beginning to haunt him. Suddenly, a horrible thought struck him: if the nameless stranger was the Devil, then the requiem must be for his own soul. . . .

A requiem is a mass—a type of Christian religious service—for the soul of someone who has died. *Requiem* is Latin for "rest." It is the first word of the mass.

A requiem may be said or sung. Many great composers, including Berlioz, Verdi, Brahms and, of course, Mozart, set the words of the requiem to music.

"Will You Miss Me?"

When she returned
home from Baden,
Constanze let out a
little scream of dismay
as she caught sight of
her husband. His skin
was yellow and blotchy,
and he had lost weight.

"My poor darling!"
she cried, throwing her
arms around his neck.
"You look so unwell!
You were supposed to
be resting!"

"I've tried to rest,"
Wolfgang explained,
"but there's always
so much to do." He grinned.
"Now that you're back, I'll get better.
I promise I will!"

But Wolfgang did not
get better. And his workload
became even heavier. Besides rehearsing
The Magic Flute and writing the *Requiem*
and other pieces, he had another new task.
The Emperor Joseph II had asked Wolfgang
to write a new opera, *The Clemency of Titus*,
to celebrate his coronation in Prague.
The fee was good. But it had to
be ready for performance
by early September.

Wolfgang composed the music for *The Clemency of Titus* in just 18 days. It was an extraordinary feat. He even worked on it in the coach that carried Constanze and himself to Prague.

The couple arrived on August 28. Constanze spent the next week enjoying the sights of the great city. Everywhere she went, she noticed that her husband's music was being played. If he was paid for every performance, she thought, we would be rich indeed.

Meanwhile, Wolfgang was dashing around madly, desperately trying to make sure that the opera was ready on time. Sometimes he was too tired and too ill to attend rehearsals.

The Clemency of Titus was performed before the emperor and empress on September 6. The grand occasion was not a success. Some said the opera was too serious; the empress said the singers were awful.

Although the opera was performed a few more times, Wolfgang did not see it. Exhausted, sick, and depressed, he and Constanze were already on their way back home.

Back in Vienna, Wolfgang continued
rehearsing *The Magic Flute* and writing the
Requiem. But his health was getting worse.

One afternoon, when they were playing
billiards, Constanze said, "I think you should see
the doctor again, my love."

"Maybe," muttered Wolfgang, concentrating
on his shot.

Constanze put her hand over the ball he was
aiming at. "Listen!" she said firmly. "You've been
sick for a long time, and you're not getting any
better. We must do something about it."

Wolfgang stood up and gave Constanze
a long, sad look. Then he said, very quietly,
"Will you miss me?"

"What are you talking about?" frowned Constanze.

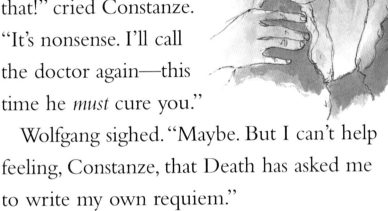

"When I'm gone— will you miss me?"

"Don't talk like that!" cried Constanze. "It's nonsense. I'll call the doctor again—this time he *must* cure you."

Wolfgang sighed. "Maybe. But I can't help feeling, Constanze, that Death has asked me to write my own requiem."

Death had not asked Mozart to write his own requiem. The mysterious visitor was actually the servant of Count Franz von Walsegg. In February 1791, the count's lovely young wife, Anna, had suddenly died. Overcome with misery, he wanted the best composer in Austria to write a requiem that could be sung every year in her memory.

First Night

Wolfgang did see the doctor again. As before, the man could not say what was wrong with the composer. Annoyed, Constanze called for a second doctor. He could not put a name to Wolfgang's illness either.

It was now late September, and the first night of *The Magic Flute* was approaching fast. With just a week to go, Wolfgang finished the last pieces of music and gave them to the orchestra.

All of the players agreed that the music was some of the best Wolfgang had ever written.

The singers were also delighted with their parts. Many of them were Wolfgang's friends. Schikaneder had even cast himself in the opera, playing the part of the bird-catcher, Papageno.

Wolfgang knew that Schikaneder's voice was not very good, so he'd kept Papageno's singing nice and simple.

On the morning of September 30, 1791, the day of *The Magic Flute's* first performance, Wolfgang was very nervous.

"What if they hate it, sweetheart?" he asked Constanze over breakfast.

"Don't be silly!" she smiled at him. "Who doesn't like the music of Wolfgang Amadeus Mozart, the finest composer in all Austria?"

Wolfgang looked at her miserably. "Is that all I am, the best in Austria?" he asked.

"Of course not!" laughed Constanze. "You're the finest in all of Europe—the whole world!"

"That's better!" grinned Wolfgang, getting up from the table. "Now the finest composer in the world is going for a walk."

By the door he paused and looked back into the room. "Constanze?"

"Yes, my love?"

"If I could feel well again, I wouldn't mind being just the second-best composer in the world. Or even the third."

With that, he left the room. The moment he was gone, Constanze burst into tears.

Almost a thousand people packed into the
Free House Theater that evening. Just before
seven o'clock, Wolfgang, dressed in a new red
coat, walked out to conduct the orchestra.

The audience cheered and whistled. Wolfgang
bowed low, then turned to his left and winked
at Constanze. The audience went quiet, he
raised his baton—and *The Magic Flute* began.

The opera was a fantastic success. The audience clapped for all of the solos and applauded loud and long after the first act. As it ended, the noise of stamping, shouting, and clapping was deafening. Flowers rained onto the stage.

Schikaneder signaled to Wolfgang to join him. The composer was so tired that he could barely walk. He staggered up the steps and stood on the stage beside the beaming Schikaneder.

The lights, the heat, and the noise were almost more than Wolfgang could bear. Although his face was smiling, inside he was crying with pain.

Schikaneder's Free House Theater had been rebuilt in 1786 and was one of the larger theaters in Vienna. Inside it was just 98 feet (30 m) long and 49 feet (15 m) wide. At the sides there were two rows of private boxes for the wealthy—it cost ten times as much to sit here. Mozart's orchestra sat in front of the stage, a wooden partition separating it from the audience.

Nearing the End

The Magic Flute was performed night after
night. But Wolfgang was strong enough to
conduct only two performances. Nevertheless,
he sometimes stopped in at the
theater with Constanze,
just to see how the
show was going.
Once, in good
spirits and not feeling
too ill, he went
backstage during
a performance.
Schikaneder, as
Papageno, had to
play magic chimes.
Actually, the instrument
on stage was a dummy. A musician played
a real glockenspiel behind the scenes.

Wolfgang whispered to the glockenspiel
player, "May I try?" The man nodded and
made way for the grinning Wolfgang.

When Schikaneder struck the dummy
chimes on stage, Wolfgang didn't play a note.
The audience snickered. Schikaneder turned
to them in astonishment. As he did so, Wolfgang
started striking the glockenspiel offstage.

Furious, Schikaneder poked his head around
the curtain, saw Wolfgang, and shouted, "Shut up!"

The audience clapped loudly and hooted
with laughter.

During November, more doctors came to see Wolfgang. They comforted but could not cure him. He was now suffering from blinding headaches and was often sick. By the end of the month he was too ill to leave the house.

Constanze was beside herself with grief and worry. "Please," she begged her husband time and again, "don't work today. Just rest."

"I must finish my requiem," Wolfgang would reply. "It's too important to leave."

Constanze wished he wouldn't call it "my requiem." It sounded as if he really was composing the music for his own funeral.

At night, while *The Magic Flute* was being performed, Wolfgang lay with a watch on the pillow beside him. That way, he could tell where the performance had gotten to. Sometimes, Constanze heard him quietly singing to himself as he followed the opera in his mind.

Based on Schikaneder's words, *The Magic Flute* was the last opera that Mozart completed. It was unlike any other opera he had composed. On the surface, it is a fairly simple, and often funny, love story. Two pairs of lovers—Tamino and Pamina, and Papageno and Papagena—have to overcome many obstacles before good conquers evil. Deeper down, the opera is full of hidden mysteries. This makes it popular with audiences of all kinds.

Finished

On the afternoon of December 3, 1791, a small group of friends gathered in the Mozarts' apartment. Wolfgang, looking deathly pale and wearing a loose robe, greeted them in his study.

"Thank you for coming," he said quietly. "As you know, I have been writing a requiem. Today, with your help, we can hear what it sounds like."

Wolfgang slowly handed out the sheets of handwritten music. The piano sounded, and the singers began: "O Lord, grant them eternal peace. . . ."

The music was splendid, but painfully sad. Wolfgang, who sang the alto part, struggled to keep going. The other singers tried not to cry.

Eventually, they came to the line, "O tearful one!" and Wolfgang could go no further. His head slumped forward, his music fell to the floor, and he broke down sobbing.

"I'm so sorry!" he wept. "But I have known all along that this is not just a requiem for one of my patrons. It is also for me!"

Wolfgang was right. No one could save him now. The next night a priest came to forgive his sins and bless him. Later, the family doctor arrived. He soon left. There was nothing more he could do.

Shortly before midnight, Wolfgang became unconscious. Constanze was almost insane with grief. Kneeling beside the bed, she sobbed, "Please, dear God, don't let him die!"

Constanze's prayers were in vain. Just before one o'clock the next morning, Wolfgang Amadeus Mozart took his last breath.

When she saw that her husband was dead, Constanze burst into hysterical tears and climbed into bed beside the corpse. She hoped to catch Wolfgang's illness and die with him.

Constanze did not die. She was, however, too upset to organize her husband's funeral. The following afternoon, after a short service in St. Stephen's Cathedral, the body of one of the greatest musical geniuses of all time was buried in an unmarked grave.

We still cannot be sure what disease Mozart died of. At the time it was called "heated military fever." This covered up the fact that doctors did not really know what was wrong with him. Nowadays, experts believe that he died of kidney disease. His condition had been made worse by his failure to rest.

Mozart's Family

Constanze Mozart soon recovered from her husband's death and made a comfortable living from his music and his reputation. In 1809 she married her lodger, Georg Nikolaus Nissen. With her help, he wrote a full biography of the great composer.

Constanze died in 1842. Her second son, Franz Xaver Wolfgang, had an unsuccessful career as a musician. His brother, Karl Thomas, became a bookkeeper. Emanuel Schikaneder ran into financial difficulties and few people noticed when he died in Vienna in 1812.

Mozart's Music

The *Requiem* was finished by Wolfgang's friend and ex-pupil, Franz Süssmayr. Count von Walsegg conducted its first performance on December 14, 1793. Since then, like all of Wolfgang's brilliant pieces, it has been performed thousands of times all over the world. *The Magic Flute* is an international favorite. It has been made into a film and translated into many languages. In 1859, a monument to Wolfgang was put up in the cemetery where he was buried. The exact position of his grave will never be known. His true monument will always be his supreme music.

Timeline

1756   January 27. Wolfgang Amadeus Mozart is born in Salzburg, Austria.

1759   Begins music lessons with his father, Leopold Mozart.

1761   Composes his first music.

1762   Goes on his first tour.

1763-66 Leopold Mozart takes his genius son on a tour around many countries.

1764   Writes his first symphony.

1767   Writes his first piano concerto.

1777   Falls in love with Aloysia Weber. She refuses to marry him.

1780   Composes music for Emanuel Schikaneder.

1782   Marries Aloysia Weber's sister, Constanze.

1784   Karl Thomas Mozart born.

1785   Begins the opera *The Marriage of Figaro*.

1787   Meets Beethoven, a promising young composer. Composing at the court of the emperor of Austria, Joseph II.

1788   Writes his last symphony.

1789   Revolution breaks out in France. Heavily in debt.

1790   Frequently ill.

1791   Franz Xaver Wolfgang Mozart is born. Writes his last piano concerto, his clarinet concerto, *The Magic Flute* (opera) and his *Requiem*. December 5, dies.

More Information

Books to read
Mozart and Classical Music
by Manuela Cappon, Francesco Salvi,
and Hans Tid, Barron's Educational
Series, 1998.
Young Mozart
by Rachel Isadora, Viking, 1997.
Mozart by Wendy Lynch,
Heinemann, 2000.
Introducing Mozart
by Roland Vernon, Silver Burdett, 2000.
Wolfgang Amadeus Mozart
by Mike Venezia, Children's Press, 1995.

Websites
http://inkpot.com/classical/mozart.html
http://w3.rz-berlin.mpg.de/cmp/
  mozart.html
You can hear Mozart's music on:
http://www.classicalarchives.com/
  mozart.html

Museums
For information about the Mozart
museums in Salzburg, Austria, contact:
Internationalen Stiftung Mozarteum,
Salzburg, Schwarzstraße 26,
A-5020 Salzburg, Austria.

Glossary

chorus A number of people singing
together.

compose To write music. A person
who composes is a composer.

concerto A piece of music played
by an orchestra and a solo instrument,
such as a piano or clarinet.

ducat A valuable coin used in
Mozart's day.

empire A group of lands governed
by one country. An emperor or
empress is head of an empire.

glockenspiel A musical instrument.
It consists of a row of bells or
metal tubes and is played with
a small hammer.

mass A service in the Roman
Catholic Church.

opera A play in which most or all
of the words are sung rather than
spoken.

orchestra Any instruments that play
together under the leadership of
a conductor.

requiem A religious service for the
soul of someone who has died.

solo A single voice singing or a
musical instrument playing on its
own, usually accompanied by an
orchestra or keyboard.

symphony A large piece of music
for an orchestra.

Index